Topic 1 Ethical research

GW00602731

Psychological research seeks to improve our understanding of human nature. Ethics are the standards that can be applied regarding issues of right or wrong.

An ethical issue occurs wi̇.... ....en how the researcher wishes to carry out meaningful research and the rights of participants.

Item 1 Ethical guidelines

The British Psychological Society (BPS) has issued a set of ethical guidelines for research involving human participants. These ethical guidelines are designed to protect the wellbeing and dignity of research participants. The following guidelines are adapted from 'Ethical principles for conducting research with human participants'. The complete text is available on the website of the British Psychological Society (**www.bps. org.uk**).

Introduction

Good psychological research is possible only if there is mutual respect and confidence between investigators and participants. Ethical guidelines are necessary to clarify the conditions under which psychological research is acceptable.

General

In all circumstances, investigators must consider the ethical implications and psychological consequences for the participants in their research and the investigation should be considered from the standpoint of all participants. Foreseeable threats to participants' psychological wellbeing, health, values or dignity should be eliminated.

Consent

Whenever possible, the investigator should inform all participants of the objectives of the investigation and of all aspects of the research that might reasonably be expected to influence willingness to participate. Where research involves any person under 16 years of age, consent should be obtained from parents or from those *in loco parentis*.

Deception

The misleading of participants is unacceptable if the participants are typically likely to object or show unease once debriefed. Intentional deception of the participants over the purpose and general nature of the investigation should be avoided whenever possible.

Debriefing

Where the participants are aware that they have taken part in an investigation, when the data have been collected the investigator should provide the participants with any necessary information to complete their understanding of the nature of the research.

Withdrawal from the investigation

At the start of the investigation, investigators should make plain to participants that they have the right to withdraw retrospectively any consent given, and to require that their own data, including recordings, be destroyed.

Confidentiality

Participants in psychological research have a right to expect that information they provide will be treated confidentially and, if published, will not be identifiable as theirs.

Protection of participants

Investigators have a responsibility to protect participants from physical and mental harm during the investigation. Where research may involve behaviour or experiences that participants may regard as personal and private, the participants must be protected from stress by all appropriate measures, including the assurance that answers to personal questions need not be given.

Observational research

Studies based upon observation must respect the privacy and psychological wellbeing of the individuals studied. Unless those observed give their consent to being observed, observational research is only acceptable in situations where those observed would expect to be observed by strangers.

Ethical research: the psychologist's dilemma
Informed consent

All participants should be asked to give informed consent prior to taking part in research. However, in some situations where deception may be used, it is not possible to obtain fully informed consent from the participants of the study.

Deception

It can be argued that if participants are not deceived about the true aims of a study their behaviour will not reflect how they would really behave in their everyday lives because they will show the effects of demand characteristics. The dilemma for researchers is to design and conduct research that accurately portrays human behaviour while at the same time ensuring that they do not breach the ethical guidelines.

Read item 1 and your textbook, then fill in the blanks in the following sentences.

1 Psychologists must protect participants from _____.

2 _____ questions are unethical to include on questionnaires.

3 _____ occurs when psychologists do not tell participants the true aim of the research.

4 _____ takes place when psychologists tell untruths to participants.

5 Participants must be reminded they can _____ from research.

6 Psychologists must not _____ their participants.

7 It is unethical to observe people's behaviour unless they are in a _____ place.

8 If psychologists are worried about the ethics of their research they should confer with _____.

9 Parents or guardians must be asked to _____ when children under 16 are to be studied.

10 Psychologists must _____ participants at the end of research procedures.

11 Psychologists take great care researching socially _____ subjects.

12 Participants must be asked for _____ consent.

13 Only when participants are told the true _____ of the study can they have given informed consent.

14 Before the research psychologists should _____ participants to make sure they understand what they will be asked to do.

Topic 2 Self report

Psychologists use many methods to conduct research. Each method has advantages and limitations, and the method selected needs to be appropriate for the topic of research. Quantitative research uses methods that measure amounts of behaviour, usually by assigning a numeric value to what is being measured (the quantity). Qualitative research measures what behaviour is like (the quality) and usually results in descriptive data.

Item 1 Interviews and questionnaires

One way to find out about people's behaviour is to ask them questions. Psychologists may use face-to-face interviews or design questionnaires to be used in surveys. However, one of the main problems about asking people questions about their behaviour is that we all like others to think well of us and, as result, what we say about our behaviour and how we actually behave may be different. Some examples of the core studies that use self-report methods to collect data are:

- Dement and Kleitman (1957) — physiological approach; laboratory experiment (REM sleep and dreaming); asked people to report what they were dreaming about
- Reicher and Haslam (2001) — social approach; experimental case study (prison); in conjunction with the BBC; used psychometric tests at the end of every day to measure group identification and stress levels
- Griffiths et al. (1994) — individual differences approach: natural (quasi) experiment: cognitive bias in regular gamblers; asked participants to 'think aloud' while playing on a fruit machine
- Freud (1909) — developmental approach; case study: Little Hans; Hans' father asked Hans to tell him about his dreams and fantasies

There are several different ways in which psychologists use self-report methods.

Structured interviews

In a structured interview all participants are asked the same questions in the same order.

Advantage: structured interviews can be replicated and can be used to compare people's responses.

Disadvantage: they can be time-consuming and require skilled researchers. People's responses can be affected by social desirability bias.

Unstructured interviews

In unstructured interviews participants can discuss anything freely and the interviewer devises new questions on the basis of answers given previously.

Advantage: unstructured interviews provide rich and detailed information but they cannot be replicated and people's responses cannot be compared.

Disadvantage: they can be time-consuming and people's responses can be affected by social desirability bias. Trained interviewers are required to carry them out.

Questionnaires

Questionnaires usually require written responses but can be conducted face to face, completed over the telephone, or on the internet. Printed questionnaires are completed by participants. They are similar to structured interviews in that all participants are asked the same questions in the same order. They usually restrict participants to a narrow range of answers.

Advantage: questionnaires are a practical way to collect a large amount of information quickly and they can be replicated.

Disadvantage: problems can arise if the questions are unclear or if they suggest a 'desirable' response, as responses can be affected by social desirability bias.

Self-report methods and ethical issues

Interviews and questionnaires: participants should not be asked embarrassing questions (protection from psychological harm) and should be reminded that they do not have to answer questions if they do not want to. Protecting confidentiality is important.

Item 2 Types of questions

Open questions

An example of an open question is:

Why did you decide to study psychology?

In response to this type of question the participant can say as much or as little as they like. The data collected may be rich and detailed and are qualitative.

Advantage: an advantage of using open questions to collect qualitative data is that we may gather detailed explanations for why people behave in the way they do.

Disadvantage: a disadvantage of using open questions to collect qualitative data is that the data are difficult to analyse, cannot be used to make statistical comparisons and may be misinterpreted by the researcher.

Closed questions

An example of a closed question is:

Do you find psychology interesting? Yes or No

In response to this type of question the participant is forced to choose one of the responses given. The data collected are quantitative.

Advantage: an advantage of using closed questions to collect quantitative data is that the data can be statistically analysed and used to make comparisons and presented in charts and graphs.

Disadvantage: a disadvantage of using closed questions to collect quantitative data is that we only know *what* people's opinions or behaviour is. We have no explanation for *why* they hold these opinions or why they behave in the way they report.

Questions using a rating scale

An example of a question using a rating scale is:

Circle the response that you most agree with.

Psychology is interesting.

Strongly agree   Agree   No opinion   Disagree   Strongly disagree

This question is an example of a five-point Likert scale. To score this question the researcher will allocate a score to each response, perhaps ranging from 1 to 5, where 5 = strongly agree and 1 = strongly disagree.

Another example of questions using a rating scale might be:

Circle the number that best reflects your opinion, where 0 = not at all, and 10 = very.

How interesting is psychology?

0 1 2 3 4 5 6 7 8 9 10

Advantage: an advantage of using questions having a rating scale is that the rating scale allows the researcher to give a numerical value to a subjective opinion, thus collecting quantitative data that can be analysed statistically, used to make comparisons and presented in charts and graphs.

Disadvantage: a disadvantage of using a rating scale is that even when two or more participants select the same 'value' it cannot be assumed that they share the same opinion. You and I may have the same opinion as to how interesting psychology is, but you might circle 7 and I might circle 9, or, in a Likert scale, you might select 'agree' and I might select 'strongly agree'. When this happens the quantitative scores may hide qualitative differences of opinion.

Read items 1 and 2 and your textbook, then answer the following questions.

1 When using the interview method, researchers may use structured or unstructured interview techniques. Explain how these differ.

....

....

....

....

....

....

2 Outline one advantage of using self-report methods to collect information.

....

....

3 A psychologist wants to investigate early child development so she designs a questionnaire asking about infants' social behaviour and gives these to mothers.
Examples of questions she asks are:

Describe how your child behaves when he/she is playing with other children.

Does your child share his/her toys willingly?   Yes or No

a Explain one advantage of using questionnaires to collect these data.

....

....

....

....

b Some of the questions collect quantitative data. Explain one advantage of collecting quantitative data.

....

....

....

c Which of the example questions is a closed question?

....

....

d Outline one advantage of using closed questions.

....

....

....

e Explain one advantage of collecting qualitative data.

....

....

....

4 A researcher is studying stress associated with driving. He plans to use the self-report method to research levels of stress in motorists who drive in the UK.

a Identify one strength and one weakness of using the self-report method in this study.

....

....

....

....

....

....

....

b Suggest an appropriate question using a rating scale that could be used in this study.

....

....

c The research found that many people reported high stress levels. Explain why we cannot conclude that people were stressed because of their driving conditions.

....

....

....

....

....

Exam-style questions

A researcher used self-report methods to find out about student friendship patterns. Twenty students were given a questionnaire to complete. Some examples of the questions appear below:

On average how many friends do you have?

Briefly describe your best friend.

Do you quarrel with your friends?   Never ☐   Sometimes ☐   Often ☐

1 Identify one open question and one closed question from this investigation.   `2 marks`

....

....

2 Outline one strength and one weakness from the closed question you have identified.   `6 marks`

....

....

....

....

....

....

3 What are qualitative data?   `2 marks`

....

....

4 Explain how qualitative data would be obtained from one of the questions used in this investigation.

3 marks

....

....

....

....

....

....

....

....

5 The table below shows the data obtained from the investigation.

Participant	Male student: number of friends	Female student: number of friends
1	4	4
2	3	5
3	5	5
4	4	4
5	4	6
6	6	6
7	3	6
8	2	5
9	4	4
10	3	4

Identify two findings from the data in this investigation.

4 marks

....

....

....

....

....

....

....

....

....

....

....

....

....

Topic 3 Experiment

You need to be able to identify, describe and evaluate three different types of experimental methods — laboratory experiments, field experiments and natural (quasi) experiments. Some examples of the core studies that use experimental methods are:

- Loftus and Palmer (1974) — cognitive approach; laboratory experiment (eye witness memory)
- Piliavin et al. (1969) — social approach; field experiment (good samaritanism)
- Bandura et al. (1961) — developmental approach; laboratory experiment (the bobo doll study)
- Baron Cohen et al. (1997) — cognitive approach; natural (quasi) experiment (recognising emotion in the eyes)
- Griffiths et al. (1994) — individual differences approach; natural (quasi) experiment; cognitive bias in regular gamblers
- Dement and Kleitman (1957) — physiological approach; laboratory experiment (REM sleep and dreaming)

Item 1 Laboratory experiments

A laboratory experiment is a method of conducting research in which researchers try to control all the variables except the one that is changed between the experimental conditions. The variable that is changed is called the **independent variable (IV)** and the effect it may have is called the **dependent variable (DV)**. So the IV is manipulated and its effect (the DV) is measured. Laboratory experiments are conducted in controlled and often artificial (not like everyday life) settings.

Advantages

- High levels of control in a laboratory experiment allow extraneous variables that might affect the IV or the DV to be minimised. The researcher can be sure that any changes in the DV are the result of changes in the IV.
- High levels of control make it possible to measure the effect of one variable on another. Statements about cause and effect can be made.
- Laboratory experiments can be replicated to check the findings with either the same or a different group of participants.

Disadvantages

- Laboratory experiments may not measure how people behave outside the laboratory in their everyday lives. Some experimental settings and tasks are artificial and contrived, thus the findings may have low internal validity.
- Aspects of the experiment may act as cues to behaviour that cause the participants (and the experimenter) to change the way they behave (demand characteristics), sometimes because of what they think is being investigated or how they think they are expected to behave. This can mean that it is not the effect of the IV that is measured, leading to invalid results.

Item 2 Field experiments

A field experiment is a way of conducting research in an everyday environment — for example, in a school or hospital — where the experimenter manipulates one or more IVs and the effect it may have (the DV) is measured.

One difference between laboratory and field experiments is an increase in the naturalness of the setting and a decrease in the level of control the experimenter is able to achieve. The key difference is the extent to which participants know they are being studied. In some field experiments, participants are aware of being studied but this is not true of most; when participants do not know they are being observed their behaviour is more natural.

Advantages

- Field experiments allow psychologists to measure how people behave in their everyday lives. The findings may have high external validity.
- Manipulation of the IV and some level of control make it possible to measure the effect of one variable on another. Statements about cause and effect can be made.
- If participants do not know they are participating in a study, they will be unaware they are being watched or manipulated. This reduces the probability that their behaviour results from demand characteristics. However this may not be true of all field experiments; the extent to which demand characteristics are

present will vary depending on the experimental setting.

Disadvantages

- It is not always possible to control for extraneous variables that might affect the IV or the DV. The researcher cannot always be sure that any changes in the DV are the result of changes in the IV.

- Field experiments can be difficult to replicate and thus it may not be possible to check the reliability of the findings.
- It may not be possible to ask participants for their informed consent, participants may be deceived and may not be debriefed, all of which are breaches of the BPS ethical guidelines.

Item 3 Natural (quasi) experiments

A natural experiment is one in which, rather than being manipulated by the researcher, the IV to be studied occurs naturally. Some examples of naturally occurring variables are gender, age, ethnicity, occupation, and smoker or non-smoker. When the IV is naturally occurring, participants cannot be randomly allocated between conditions. A natural experiment may take place in a laboratory or in a field experimental setting.

Advantages

- Natural experiments allow psychologists to study the effects of IVs that could be unethical to manipulate.

- When participants are unaware of the experiment, and the task is not contrived, research may have high internal validity.

Disadvantages

- Since participants cannot be allocated randomly between conditions, it is possible that other variables (individual differences other than the IV) can also affect the DV. This may lead to low internal validity.
- Natural experiments can be difficult to replicate with a different group of participants, thus it may not be possible to check the reliability of the findings.

Item 4 Ethical issues

Laboratory experiment

Even when told they have the right to withdraw, participants may feel reluctant to do so and may feel they should do things they would not normally do. Participants may be deceived.

Field experiment

It may be difficult to obtain informed consent and participants may not be able to withdraw. It may be difficult to debrief the participants.

Natural experiment

Confidentiality may be a problem because the sample studied may be identifiable. Where naturally occurring social variables are studied (e.g. family income, ethnicity), ethical issues may arise when drawing conclusions and publishing the findings.

Read items 1–3 and your textbook, then answer the following questions.

1 Fill in the blank spaces.

a This type of experiment takes place in specially contrived settings. _____

b This type of experiment may take place in work places or schools. _____

c In this type of experiment the IV is a natural occurrence. _____

d In this type of experiment it is hard to control variables other than the IV. _____

e In this type of experiment individual differences other than the IV may be hard to control. _____

f This type of data are easy to analyse so we can make comparisons. _____

g This type of data tend to be subjective (opinion based) but are rich in detail.

_____

h The moral rules set out to ensure that psychologists do not harm their participants.

_____

i This is what is manipulated in an experiment. _____

j This is what is measured in an experiment. _____

k These are used to try to ensure that only the IV can affect the DV in an experiment.

_____

l Closed questions collect _____ data.

m Open questions collect _____ data.

2 Describe one difference between a laboratory experiment and a field experiment.

....
....
....
....
....

3 Outline one advantage and one disadvantage of laboratory experiments.

....
....
....
....

4 Outline one advantage and one disadvantage of using the field experiment method.

....
....
....
....
....
....

5 What is the defining characteristic of a natural experiment?

....

....

....

....

Exam-style questions

Planning consent has been granted for a supermarket to be built near your school. There are two psychology classes and teachers worry that the students whose classroom is next to the noisy building site will be distracted and will learn less than those whose classroom is on the quiet side of the school. They decide to conduct research into the effect of the building-site noise. They design a test to be administered to the 'noisy' and 'quiet' side students. The test is on the core studies; it comprises 20 questions and each correct answer scores one point.

1 Identify the research method used in this experiment and suggest one weakness of this research method.   **4 marks**

....

....

....

2 Identify the IV and the DV in this experiment.   **4 marks**

....

....

....

3 Suggest whether the data collected in this experiment are quantitative or qualitative.   **2 marks**

....

....

4 Suggest two variables that would be difficult for the teachers to control.   **4 marks**

....

....

....

5 Identify one ethical issue that would arise in the research and suggest how the researchers could deal with this.   **3 marks**

....

....

....

....

Topic 4 Research design

When planning research it is important to consider the design of the research. You need to be able to describe and evaluate independent measures design, repeated measures design and matched participants (subjects) design.

Item 1 Types of research design

Independent measures design

In an experiment having an independent measures design, different participants are used in each of the experimental (research) conditions.

Advantages: no participants are 'lost' between trials; participants can be randomly allocated between the conditions to distribute individual differences evenly; there are no practise effects.

Disadvantages: it needs more participants; there may be important differences between the groups to start with that are not removed by the random allocation of participants between conditions.

Repeated measures design

In an experiment having a repeated measures design, the same group of participants is used in each of the conditions.

Advantages: it requires fewer participants; it controls for individual differences between participants because, in effect, the participants are compared against themselves.

Disadvantages: it cannot be used in studies in which participation in one condition will affect responses in another (e.g. where participants learn tasks); it cannot be used in studies where an **order effect** would create a problem. An order effect reduces internal validity.

One way that researchers control for order effects is to use **counterbalancing**. Half the participants complete condition A followed by condition B, the other half complete condition B followed by condition A. In this way, any order effects are balanced out.

Matched participants (subjects) design

Separate groups of participants are used who are matched on a one-to-one basis using characteristics such as age, sex or IQ, to control, as far as possible, any individual differences that may affect what is being measured.

Advantages: matching participants controls for some individual differences; it can be used when a repeated measures design is not appropriate — for example, when performing the task twice would result in a practise effect.

Disadvantages: a large number of prospective participants are needed from which to select matched pairs, and it is difficult to match on some characteristics (for example, personality); more participants are needed than in a repeated measures design.

Read item 1 and your textbook, then answer the following questions.

A researcher is carrying out an experiment to find out whether people recall more items from a list of 20 words when they learn it in a quiet room or when they learn it in a room in which loud music is playing. Forty psychology students were randomly allocated to the two conditions. The 20 words were all names of animals, flowers or trees.

1 Identify the independent variable and the dependent variable in this study.

....

....

....

2 Explain whether this is an independent design or a repeated measures design.

....

....

3 Explain one advantage of using a repeated measures design in this research.

....

....

....

4 Describe and evaluate an appropriate procedure for this study.

....

....

....

....

....

....

....

....

....

....

....

....

....

....

....

....

....

....

....

....

....

....

Topic 5 Observation

When psychologists conduct observations, they watch and record people's behaviour but usually remain inconspicuous and do nothing to change or interfere with the behaviour they observe. It is important to remember that when using experimental methods, researchers may choose to use observation to collect data.

Participant observations: the observer becomes part of the situation he/she is observing.

Naturalistic observations: the observer stays hidden from the people whose behaviour is being observed.

Some examples of core studies that used observational methods to collect data are:

- Bandura et al. (1961) — developmental approach; laboratory experiment (the bobo doll study); used covert time sampled observation to record the children's aggressive behaviour
- Rosenhan (1973) — individual differences approach; field experiment ('On being sane in insane places'); used participant observation to record the behaviour on psychiatric wards
- Milgram (1963) — social approach; laboratory experiment having no IV (obedience); observed the signs of stress and distress in the behaviour of the participants

Item 1 Observational methods
Sampling observational data

Sometimes observations are made continuously where the observer records everything that happens in detail, perhaps using a video camera. More often, researchers use a **sampling technique** because it might be difficult to record everything. Two observational sampling techniques are **event sampling** and **time sampling**.

- Event sampling means that observations are made of specific events or occurrences that have been defined or categorised previously and the researcher records an event every time it is observed — for example, ticking a tally chart every time someone uses a mobile phone. However, if too many of the 'behaviours of interest' happen at once, it may be difficult to record everything.
- Time sampling occurs when the researcher decides how long the observation will last, and decides on a time frame, say every 30 seconds, and then records what behaviours occur in every 30 second time frame. Time sampling means that the observations are made for specific lengths of time — for example, every 2 minutes over a 1-hour period. There is usually more than one observer in a time-sampled observation. (Data were gathered by a time-sampled observation in the Bandura 'bobo' doll experiment, for example.)

Inter-observer reliability

Inter-observer reliability (or inter-rater reliability) is the extent to which we can be sure that all observers are 'counting' the behaviours in the same way when there is more than one observer. A pilot study can be conducted and then a check is carried out to see that all observers have the same behaviour scores.

Advantages of observational methods

- Behaviour can be observed in its usual setting and usually there are no problems with demand characteristics unless the situation in which the participants are being observed has been specially contrived.
- It is useful when researching children or animals.
- It can be a useful way to gather data for a pilot study.

Disadvantages of observational methods

- No explanation for the observed behaviour is gained because the observer counts instances of behaviour but does not ask participants to explain why they acted as they did.
- Observers may 'see what they expect to see' (observer bias) or may miss, or misinterpret, behaviour.
- Naturalistic observations are difficult to replicate.
- Inter-observer reliability must be established when there is more than one observer, but this may be difficult to establish.

Naturalistic observations and ethical issues

If informed consent is not being gained, people should only be observed in public places and where they would not be distressed to find they were being observed. If the location in which behaviour was observed is identifiable, an ethical issue may arise in terms of protecting confidentiality.

Read item 1 and your textbook, then answer the following questions.

Researchers wanted to undertake an observational study of aggression in toddlers. They went to a nursery school and observed 30 children at play.

1 Suggest three types of aggression that could be categorised for this observation.

....

....

....

2 Outline one advantage and one disadvantage of research using naturalistic observation for this research.

....

....

....

....

....

....

....

....

....

....

....

3 Identify one ethical issue arising from this research and explain how this issue might be dealt with.

....

....

....

....

....

....

Exam-style questions

You are planning to carry out observational research looking at how students use mobile phones. You and a friend carry out an observation of a group of students for about an hour.

1 List two categories of behaviour you might observe in this study.   `2 marks`

....

....

2 Briefly describe a suitable procedure for this observational study. **5 marks**

3 Explain whether you would use event sampling or time sampling in this study. **4 marks**

4 Explain how you would ensure that this observation has inter-observer reliability. **4 marks**

Topic 6 Correlation

Some examples of the core studies that use correlational methods to collect data are:

- Dement and Kleitman (1957) — physiological approach; laboratory experiment (REM sleep and dreaming); measured the correlation between how long the sleeper had been in REM sleep and the reported length of time of the dream.

- Maguire (2000) — physiological approach; natural experiment (quasi); measured the correlation between length of time spent driving a London taxi and structural changes in the hippocampus.

Item 1 Correlational research

Correlation is a statistical technique used to calculate the correlation coefficient in order to quantify the strength of relationship between two variables. An example might be whether there is a relationship between aggressive behaviour and playing violent video games. Studies that use correlational analysis cannot draw conclusions about cause and effect because if a relationship is found between behaving aggressively and playing violent video games, individual differences in personality variables could be one factor that causes both of these. Just because two events (or behaviours) co-occur does not mean that one necessarily causes the other

The correlation coefficient is a mathematical measure of the degree of relatedness between two sets of data where two scores have been gained from each participant.

Analysing correlational data

Data can be plotted as points on a scattergraph. A line of best fit is then drawn through the points to show the trend of the data.

- If both variables increase together, this is a positive correlation.
- If one variable increases as the other decreases, this is a negative correlation.
- If no line of best fit can be drawn, there is no correlation.

Correlation coefficients have a value between –1 and +1.

- A **perfect positive correlation**, indicated by +1, is where variable Y increases with variable X.
- A **perfect negative correlation**, indicated by –1, is where variable Y increases as variable X decreases.

Advantages

- Correlational analysis allows researchers to calculate the strength of a relationship between variables as a quantitative measure. A correlation coefficient of +0.9 indicates a strong positive correlation; a correlation coefficient of –0.4 indicates a weak negative correlation.
- Where a correlation is found, it is possible to make predictions about one variable from the other.
- Correlation is useful as a pointer for more detailed research.

Disadvantages

- Researchers cannot assume that one variable causes the other.
- Correlation between variables may be misleading and can be misinterpreted.
- A lack of correlation may not mean there is no relationship, because the relationship could be non-linear. For example, there is a relationship between physiological arousal and performance but the relationship is expressed by a curve, not by a straight line. The Yerkes-Dodson curve shows that performance improves under a little arousal but too much arousal reduces performance.

Correlational studies and ethics

Ethical issues can arise when researching relationships between socially sensitive variables (for example, ethnicity and IQ) because published results can be misinterpreted as suggesting 'cause and effect'.

Read item 1 and your textbook, then answer the following questions.

1 Explain what a 'negative correlation' between two variables means.

....

....

....

....

2 Which graphical technique should be used to display a correlation?

....

....

3 Outline one disadvantage of correlational methodology.

....

....

....

....

....

4 A teacher wonders whether there is a relationship between the number of lessons that students attend and the marks they are awarded in exams. The table shows the data she found for ten students.

Number of lessons attended	21	18	13	6	8	17	17	15	12	10
Marks in exam	40	55	40	25	29	45	30	45	35	15

a Draw a scattergraph to show the relationship between number of lessons attended and marks in the exam.

b What type of relationship between number of lessons attended and marks in the exam is suggested by your scattergraph?

....

....

c 'If you do not attend all my lessons you will fail your exams.'

Referring to your scattergraph, explain why this may not be a valid conclusion for the teacher to draw.

....

....

....

....

....

Exam-style questions

Researchers wanted to find out whether there was a correlation between the amount of sleep people have and verbal ability. First, participants were asked to report how much sleep they had the previous night in hours and minutes. Then, to measure verbal ability, participants were given 1 minute to say out loud as many words beginning with 's' as they could (for example, sheep, ship, sand, sun, sausage). The researcher counted the words and noted the total number.

1 Write an appropriate null hypothesis for this study.   **4 marks**

....

....

....

2 Outline one strength and one weakness of the way verbal ability was measured in this study.   **6 marks**

....

....

....

....

....

3 Explain what is meant by a positive correlation.   **2 marks**

....

....

4 Explain one advantage of using correlational methods in this research.   **3 marks**

....

....

In this topic, you will learn how psychologists formulate hypotheses and operationalise research variables. You will also learn about techniques for assessing and improving the validity and reliability of research.

Item 1 Aims and hypotheses

Research aims

The research aim is a general statement of the purpose of the study and should make clear what the study intends to investigate, but is not precise enough to test.

Hypotheses

A hypothesis states precisely what the researcher believes to be true about the target population. It is often generated from a theory and is a testable statement.

Alternative hypothesis

The alternative hypothesis states that some difference (or effect) will occur; that the independent variable (IV) does have a significant effect on the dependent variable (DV).

The null hypothesis

This is a statement of no difference or of no correlation. The null hypothesis states that the IV does not affect the DV.

Accepting or rejecting hypotheses

If data analysis forces the researcher to reject the null hypothesis because a significant effect is found, then the alternative hypothesis is accepted.

Directional or non-directional hypotheses

The alternative hypothesis can be directional or non-directional. A **directional** hypothesis is termed a 'one-tailed hypothesis' because it predicts the direction in which the results are expected to go. Directional hypotheses are used when previous research evidence suggests that it is possible to make a clear prediction about the way in which the IV will affect the DV.

A **non-directional** hypothesis is termed a 'two-tailed hypothesis' because, although researchers predict that the IV does affect the DV, they are not sure how.

Item 2 Operationalisation and control of variables

In experimental research the variable that is manipulated is called the independent variable (IV). The IV should be the only difference between the experimental conditions. The variable that is measured is called the dependent variable (DV).

The term 'operationalisation' means being able to define variables in order to manipulate the IV and measure the DV. However, some variables are easier to operationalise than others. For example, 'memory' might be operationalised as 'the number of words remembered from a list of 20 words', but it is more difficult to operationalise how stressed someone may be. You could operationalise stress by measuring physiological arousal, or you could ask participants to rate how stressed they are. When planning a research study, both the IV and the DV need to be operationalised precisely and clearly. If variables are not operationalised, the research cannot be replicated because another researcher would not be able to repeat the same measurements.

Control of variables

Any variables that change between the conditions, other than the IV, are difficult to control (for example, how tired the participants are) and are a nuisance because these variables and other environmental variables (such as the time of day a study is carried out) may affect what is being measured (the DV). In addition, standardised instructions and procedures should be used so that all participants are told what to do in exactly the same way and are treated in exactly the same way.

Research is expensive in terms of both time and money and no piece of research is perfect. To establish whether the research plan works, that participants can understand the instructions, that nothing has been missed out and that participants are able to do what is asked, a **pilot study** (a trial run with a small number of participants) should be carried out so that researchers can make adjustments and save wasting valuable resources.

Item 3 Evaluating the reliability and validity of research

Reliability

Reliability of results means consistency. In other words, if something is measured more than once, the same effect should result. If my tape measure tells me I am 152 cm tall one day but 182 cm tall the next, then the tape measure I am using is not reliable.

Internal reliability refers to how consistently a method measures within itself — for example, my tape measure should measure the same distance between 0 cm and 10 cm as it does between 10 cm and 20 cm. To test for internal reliability, researchers may use the **split-half technique** in which half of the scores are compared with the other half to see how similar they are.

External reliability refers to the consistency of measures over time (i.e. if repeated). For example, personality tests should not give different results if the same person is tested more than once. External reliability can be tested by the **test–retest method**. For example, the same participants can be tested on more than one occasion to see whether their results remain similar.

Inter-observer reliability is whether the codings or ratings of several observers in an observational study agree with each other. To improve reliability, all observers must have clear and operationalised categories of behaviour and must be trained how to use the system. Inter-observer reliability can be measured using correlational analysis, in which a high positive correlation among ratings indicates that high inter-observer reliability has been established.

Validity

Validity refers to the extent to which a measurement technique measures what it is supposed to measure.

Internal validity concerns whether the IV really caused the effect on the DV, or whether some other factor was responsible. Experiments may lack internal validity because of demand characteristics, participant reactivity, or because 'nuisance' variables have not been controlled.

Another aspect of internal validity is **mundane realism**, that is, do the measures used generalise to real life? For example, does a measure of long-term memory based on remembering lists of words generalise to how people remember past events? Mundane realism is an aspect of internal validity that contributes to external validity.

External (ecological) validity refers to the validity of a study outside the research situation and provides some idea of the extent to which the findings can be generalised to people's everyday lives. To assess the external validity of research, three factors should be considered:

- How representative of the population to which the results are to be generalised is the sample of participants (population validity)?
- Do the research setting and situation generalise to a realistic real-life setting or situation (ecological validity)?
- Do the findings generalise to the past and to the future (ecological or historical validity)? For example, it is argued that 50 years ago people were more conformist and obedient.

Read items 1–3 above and review the items in previous topics, then answer the following questions.

1 Fill in the blank spaces.

a Research has internal _____ when we can be sure that only the IV has affected what is being measured.

b Research has low _____ when uncontrolled variables can affect what is being measured.

c _____ data are an advantage because they explain why people behave in the way they do.

d Experimental research is _____ when standardised procedures are used so that the study can be repeated with a different sample.

e Research is only _____ when all the BPS guidelines have been followed.

f When repeated research finds the same result, the results are said to be

_____ .

g _____ data are an advantage because they can be analysed statistically in order to make comparisons between sets of results.

h _____ validity is achieved when research procedures have high everyday 'realism'.

i _____ are used to increase the validity of the research.

j The _____ hypothesis predicts that an IV will have no effect on what is being measured.

k A _____ correlation is when a variable increases with another increasing variable.

l A _____ is used to display the findings of correlational research.

Some research suggests that ageing may have a negative effect on memory. You carry out a research project to find out whether students have better memories than teachers. Each student or teacher is given a list of 20 words to memorise in 1 minute and then given a minute to write down as many words as they can recall.

2 Outline your research aim.

....
....
....
....

3 Identify the research method you will use and explain why you chose this method.

....
....
....
....

4 Write a testable one-tailed alternative hypothesis for your study and explain why this hypothesis is one tailed.

....
....
....
....

5 Write a testable two-tailed alternate hypothesis for your study and explain why this hypothesis is two tailed.

....

....

....

....

6 Write a null hypothesis for your study.

....

....

7 Identify the IV in your study and describe how you will operationalise it.

....

....

....

8 Identify the DV in your study and describe how you will operationalise it.

....

....

....

9 Identify one research design you could use in the study and explain, in terms of the advantages of the design, why you chose this research design?

....

....

....

....

10 Identify one environmental variable that you think will be important to control in the study you designed.

....

....

....

11 Explain why you think controlling this factor will be important.

....

....

....

....

....

Topic 8 The participants in research

When researchers conduct research, the target population is the group of people to whom they wish to generalise their findings. The sample of participants is the group of people who take part in the study, and a representative sample is a sample of people who are representative of the target population. The most frequently used sampling techniques are opportunity sampling, volunteer (self selected) sampling and random sampling. You need to be able to describe and evaluate all these sampling techniques.

Item 1 Sampling techniques

Opportunity sampling

This involves asking whoever is available and willing to participate. An opportunity sample is not likely to be representative of any target population because it will probably comprise friends of the researcher, or students, or people in a specific workplace. The people approached will be those who are local and available and they are likely to comprise a biased sample of participants who are not representative of any wider population. A sample of participants approached in the street is *not* a random sample of the population of a town. To be a random sample, all the people living in a town would have an equal opportunity to participate. In an opportunity sample, only the people present at the time the researcher was seeking participants would be able to participate.

Advantage: the researchers can quickly and inexpensively acquire a sample, and face-to-face ethical briefings and debriefings can be undertaken.

Disadvantage: opportunity samples are almost always biased samples, because who participates depends on who is asked and who happens to be available at the time.

Volunteer sampling (self selecting)

Volunteer samples mean exactly that: people who volunteer to participate. A volunteer sample may not be representative of the target population because there may be differences between the sort of people who volunteer and those who do not.

Advantage: the participants should have given their informed consent, will be interested in the research and may be less likely to withdraw.

Disadvantage: a volunteer sample may be a biased sample that is not representative of the target population because volunteers may be different in some way to non-volunteers. For example, they may be more helpful (or more curious) than non-volunteers.

Random sampling

This involves having the names of the target population and giving everyone an equal chance of being selected. A random sample can be selected by a computer or, in a small population, by selecting names from a hat.

Advantage: a true random sample avoids bias, as every member of the target population has an equal chance of being selected.

Disadvantage: it is almost impossible to obtain a truly random sample because not all the names of the target population may be known.

Item 2 Sample representativeness

Researchers want to apply the findings of their research to learn and explain something about the behaviour of the target population. Thus the sample of participants should be a true representation of diversity in the target population. In psychological research the participants are often students, but an all-student sample is only representative of a target population of students. Likewise, an all-male sample may only be representative of an all-male target population. If the sample is not representative, the research findings cannot be generalised to the target population.

Researchers also need to decide how many participants are needed. The number required depends on several factors:
- The sample must be large enough to be representative of the target population.
- If the target population is small, it may be possible,

and sensible, to use the whole population as the sample. However it is unlikely that such a small target population would be the subject of a psychology study.

■ The sample needs to be a manageable size because too many participants make research expensive and time-consuming.

■ If the research has important implications, such as research which tests a new drug, then the sample size should be larger than it would be in a less important study. In small samples, the individual differences between participants will have a greater effect. If the effect being studied is likely to be small, then a larger sample will be required.

Item 3 The relationship between researchers and participants

In any research project the interaction between researchers and participants needs to be considered. Problems can arise because of the behaviour of the researcher or of the participants.

Participant effects

When people know they are being studied, their behaviour is affected. Regardless of other variables, as soon as people know their behaviour is of interest it is likely to change. Some of the ways in which participation in research can affect behaviour are:

■ The **Hawthorne effect**: if people are aware that they are being studied, they are likely to try harder on tasks and pay more attention. This may mean that any findings (e.g. response times) are artificially high, which may lead to invalid conclusions.

■ **Demand characteristics**: sometimes, features of the research situation, the research task (and possibly the researcher) may give cues to participants as to what is expected of them or how they are expected to behave, or in some way change participants' behaviour. This may lead to response bias in which participants try to please the experimenter (or deliberately do the opposite), in which case conclusions drawn from the findings may be invalid.

■ **Social desirability bias**: people usually try to show themselves in the best possible way. So, for example, when answering questions in interviews or questionnaires they may give answers that are socially acceptable but not truthful. For example,

people tend to under-report antisocial behaviour, such as alcohol consumption and smoking, and over-report pro-social behaviour, such as giving to charity. If questions asked as part of a research project have answers that might be perceived as more or less socially desirable, it is important to be aware that answers might not be truthful and that the conclusions drawn from the findings may be invalid.

Investigator and experimenter effects

Researchers may unwittingly affect the results of their research in several ways:

■ **Investigator expectancy**: the expectations of the researcher can affect how they design their research and bias how and what they decide to measure, and how the findings are analysed.

■ **Experimenter bias**: the experimenter can affect the way participants behave. One way to reduce experimenter effects is to use a **double-blind procedure** in which neither the experimenter nor the participants know what the research hypothesis is.

■ **Interviewer effects**: the expectations of the interviewer may lead them to ask only those questions in which they are interested, or to ask leading questions, or they may only focus on answers that match their expectations.

■ **Observer bias**: when observing behaviour, observers may make biased interpretations of the meaning of behaviour.

Read items 1–3 and your textbook, then answer the following questions.

1 Complete these sentences:

a A sample is only a random sample when...

....

....

b A sample is an opportunity sample when...

....

....

c A representative sample means that...

d A sample is said to be biased when the participants...

e A large sample is needed when...

f In a small sample, the findings may be invalid because...

g A matched sample can increase the validity of the findings because .....

2 In a survey investigating students' drinking habits, explain why social desirability bias may affect the students' responses to questions about their alcohol consumption.

3 You are designing a research project to find out whether students read more books than teachers.

a Describe the population you are going to study.

b Identify a sampling technique you could use to obtain participants for this study and explain one weakness with this sampling technique.

c Suggest one reason why a volunteer sample might result in a biased sample in this study.

....

....

....

d Identify the IV in your study and describe how you would operationalise it.

....

....

e Identify the DV in your study and describe how you would operationalise it.

....

....

....

f Explain what is meant by a demand characteristic.

....

....

....

Exam-style questions

Read your textbook and then review all the previous topics and items 1–3 above.

Researchers conducted a repeated measures design experiment to find out whether brief physical exercise can reduce exam stress. The experiment took place in a local college. Posters were put up asking for interested students to come to the sports hall on Wednesday morning at 10.00 a.m. The first 20 students to turn up were asked to rate, on a scale from 1 to 10, how anxious or relaxed they were feeling (where 1 was very anxious and 10 was very relaxed). The students were then asked to jog or run around the sports hall for a distance of 100 metres. Immediately afterwards, the students were again asked to rate, on the same scale, how anxious or relaxed they were feeling.

1 Identify the sampling technique used to obtain participants for this study and suggest one weakness with it. **3 marks**

....

....

....

....

2 What is a repeated measures design? **2 marks**

....

....

....

3 Write a testable one-tailed alternative hypothesis for your study and explain why this hypothesis is one tailed.

4 marks

....

....

....

....

4 Identify one control that could have been used in this study and explain why this control would have been needed.

3 marks

....

....

....

5 Outline one strength and one weakness of using self report to measure the dependent variable (DV) in this study.

6 marks

....

....

....

....

....

....

....

Topic 9 Data analysis and presentation

In this topic you learn how to analyse data and how to present data in research reports. You need to know how to collect and record data, and how to analyse data using descriptive statistics and calculation of measures of central tendency and dispersion. You also need to be able to interpret correlational data and to be able to select the appropriate way to present data using charts and graphs.

Item 1 Data derived from observations, interviews and questionnaires

Observations, interviews and questionnaires can result in qualitative and/or quantitative data. In interviews and observations, qualitative data might result from video or audio recordings or written notes. Likewise, qualitative data can result when open questions are asked in interviews or questionnaires, or when participants are invited to explain why they behave in a certain way. It is important when analysing qualitative data that researchers avoid subjective or biased misinterpretations. Misinterpretation can be avoided by:

- using accurate language to operationalise the variables to be measured — for example, if observing play-fighting in children, an operationalised definition might be 'hitting while smiling' (though counting the frequency of this would be quantitative data)
- using a team of observers who have verified that they have achieved inter-observer reliability
- converting qualitative data into quantitative data; one way to do this is by coding the data

Coding qualitative data

- A sample of qualitative data is collected, for example from the interviewee, from magazines or newspapers, or from the notes or recordings of an observation.
- Coding units are identified in order to categorise the data. A coding unit could be specific words or phrases that are looked for (the operationalised definitions).
- The coding units may then be counted to see how frequently they occur. The resulting frequency of occurrence is a form of quantitative data.

Qualitative data

Advantages: rich and detailed; collected in real-life settings; can be used to collect data on attitudes, opinions and beliefs.

Disadvantages: may be subjective; can be an imprecise measure; may be low in reliability.

Quantitative data

Advantages: objective, precise measures used; data are high in reliability and it is possible to see patterns in the data.

Disadvantages: may lack or lose detail; often collected in contrived settings.

Item 2 Types of data

You need to be able to identify different types of data so that you can decide how best to analyse the research findings.

Nominal level data

Nominal level data are the frequencies of occurrence. For example:

- how many cars are red, how many are green, how many are blue
- how many people are left handed, how many are right handed

Use the **mode** (the most common value in the data group) as the measure of central tendency.

It makes no sense to calculate the mean because, for example, you cannot have 2.4 children, or the average of five red cars and two yellow cars.

Ordinal level data

Ordinal level data can be ranked in order, such as first, second, third. For example:
Scores = 1, 3, 4, 6, 8, 9, 11, 15, 50

Use the **median** (middle score) as the measure of central tendency because extreme scores can affect the mean.

Interval level data

Interval level data are measured on a fixed scale. Examples are height in inches, weight in grams and temperature:
13.1, 15.2, 16.2, 17.2, 18.2, 19.5

Use the **mean** (mathematical mid-point) as the measure of central tendency because this gives a precise measure of the central tendency — but remember that the mean can be affected by extreme scores.

Item 3 Descriptive statistics

Descriptive statistics describe research findings. Measures of central tendency and dispersion are used to summarise large amounts of data into typical or average values, and to provide information on the variability or spread of the scores.

Measures of central tendency

There are three ways to calculate the average of a set of scores: the mean, the median and the mode.

Mean

All the scores are added up and the total is divided by the number of scores. For example, take the following set of scores:

1 2 2 3 3 4 5 5 7 8

The mean of this set of scores is 4:
(1 + 2 + 2 + 3 + 3 + 4 + 5 + 5 + 7 + 8 = 40, divided by 10 — the number of scores).

Advantages: the mean is a sensitive measure; it takes all the values from the raw scores into account.

Disadvantages: the mean can give a distorted impression if there are unusual scores (extremely high or low) in the data set. Often, the mean may have a meaningless decimal point that was not in the original scores — for example, 2.4 children.

Median

The central score in a list of rank-ordered scores. In an odd number of scores, the median is the middle number. In an even numbered set of scores, the median is the mid-point between the two middle scores. For example, take the following set of ten scores:

2 3 4 5 5 6 7 8 15 16

The median of this set of scores is 5 + 6 divided by 2 = 5.5.

The mean of this set of scores is 7.1 (71 divided by 10).

Advantages: the median is not affected by extreme scores; it is useful when scores are ordered data (1st, 2nd, 3rd etc.).

Disadvantages: the median does not take account of the values of all of the scores and can be misleading if used in small sets of scores.

Mode

The score that occurs most frequently in a set of scores. For example, take the following set of scores:

4 4 4 4 5 6 10 12 12 14

The mode of this set of scores is 4 because it occurs four times (the most frequently).

The median of this set of scores is 5 + 6 divided by 2 = 5.5.

The mean of this set of scores is 7.5 (75 divided by 10).

This example shows that each of the measures of central tendency may describe the mid-point of a set of scores differently.

Advantages: extreme scores do not affect the mode; it may make more sense.

Disadvantages: the mode tells us nothing about other scores; there may be more than one mode in a set of data.

Measures of dispersion

Measures of dispersion tell us about the **range** of the scores, that is, how spread out they are. The range of a set of scores is calculated as the highest score minus the lowest score.

Advantage: they are easy and quick to work out and include extreme values.

Disadvantage: they may be misleading when there are extremely high or low scores in a set.

Item 4 Graphs and charts

Psychologists use graphs and charts to summarise their data in visual displays. Information provided in graphs and charts makes it easier for other people to understand the findings of research.

Scattergraphs

Scattergraphs are used to show the result of correlational analysis. You can see at a glance whether there appears to be a positive, negative or no correlation.

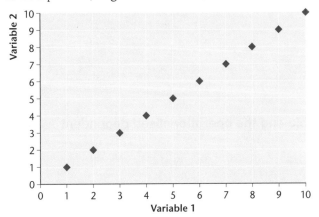

Scattergraph showing a positive correlation

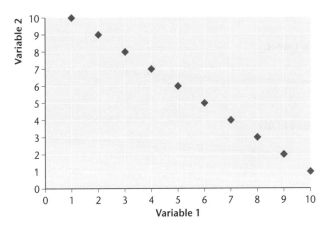

Scattergraph showing a negative correlation

Bar charts

Bar charts are used when scores are in categories, when there is no fixed order for the items on the *y*-axis, or can be used to show a comparison of means. The bar chart below shows the holiday destinations chosen by a sample of 300 families.

The bars in bar charts should be the same width **but do not touch**. The space between the bars illustrates that the variable on the *x*-axis is discrete data.

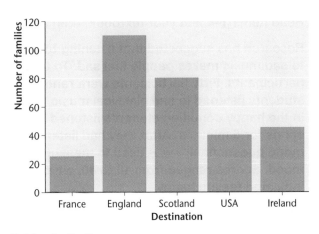

Holiday destinations

Histograms

Histograms (frequency diagrams) show frequencies using columns. Histograms should be used to display frequency distributions of continuous data and there should be no gaps between the bars. This example shows the exam results (marks) for a class of 30 students in a mock exam marked out of a maximum of 100. The scores have been grouped into ranges of 10 marks.

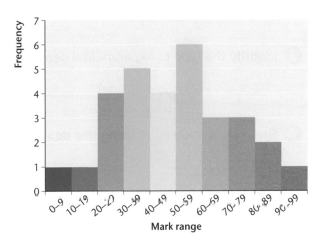

Distribution of marks in a mock exam

Read items 1–4 and your textbook, then answer the following questions.

Research has suggested that listening to happy music can cheer people up but listening to sad music makes people feel sad. To test this idea, psychologists advertised for student participants. Fifty participants were randomly allocated to two conditions. In the sad condition, students listened to sad classical music for 5 minutes, and in the happy condition students listened to jolly Christmas songs for 5 minutes. After they had listened to the music, a mood questionnaire was used to measure the participants' mood. Scores ranged from 10 to 40, where high scores indicated feeling happy.

Condition	Mean	Range
Sad music	23	6
Happy music	31	10

1 State the aim of this research.

....

....

2 Describe the operationalised independent variable and the operationalised dependent variable for this experiment.

....

....

....

....

....

3 Identify the type of experimental design that was used.

....

....

4 Give one weakness of using this design in this research.

....

....

....

....

....

5 Explain one advantage of collecting quantitative data in this research.

....

....

....

....

6 Give one advantage of using the mean to analyse the data in this research.

....

....

....

....

7 Draw a suitably labelled diagram to depict the findings of this research.

8 Give one conclusion that can be derived from your diagram. Hint: write the conclusion in terms of the research aim.

....

....

....

....

9 This study used the experimental method. Describe briefly how you could use a method other than an experimental method to investigate the same aims.

....

....

....

....

Exam-style questions

Read your textbook and review all previous items, then answer the following questions.

1 A psychologist wanted to find out whether the temperature of the classroom affects student performance in exams. To do this she devised a maths test in which the maximum score was 100. She divided a class of twenty 17 year olds into two groups. One group completed the test in a warm room while the other group completed the test in a cold room.

    a Identify which level of data are being collected.   `2 marks`

....

....

b Identify one variable, other than the temperature of the room, that might affect the results and explain why. [3 marks]

....

....

....

....

c Suggest how the researcher could control the variable you have identified. [3 marks]

....

....

....

....

d Explain one advantage of using the median to analyse the data in this research. [3 marks]

....

....

....

....

e Describe and evaluate an appropriate procedure for this study. [10 marks]

....

....

....

....

....

....

....

....

....

....

....

....

....

....

....

....

2 Researchers decided to conduct a laboratory experiment, using an independent design, to find out whether playing word games can improve memory. They put up posters asking for university students to participate in a study of memory. When a sample of 30 had been obtained the students were randomly allocated to two conditions. In the control condition the students came to the psychology laboratory and were given a list of 25 words to memorise in 2 minutes. The words were all names of rivers and trees. After the students had memorised the words, they were given 1 minute to write down as many words as they could remember. In the experimental condition participants came to the psychology laboratory and played Scrabble, in groups of four, for 1 hour every day for a week. At the end of the week they were given the same memory test.

a Identify the sampling technique used to obtain participants for this study and suggest one weakness with it. **4 marks**

b What is an independent design? **2 marks**

c Identify two controls that could have been used in this study and explain why these would have been needed. **6 marks**

d Identify the dependent variable (DV) in this study.

2 marks

....

....

....

e Outline one strength and one weakness of the way that the dependent variable (DV) has been measured in this study.

6 marks

....

....

....

....

....

....

....

....

....

f Write an appropriate alternative hypothesis for this study.

4 marks

....

....

....

....

g Identify the type of data collected in this study and suggest how you would analyse the data.

4 marks

....

....

....

....

....

The case study method

In G541 you probably won't be asked questions about the case study method, but you do need to be able to describe and evaluate this method.

A case study is a detailed study into the life and background of one person (or of a small group of people). Case studies involve looking at past records, such as school and health records, and asking other people about the participant's past and present behaviour. Case studies are often done on people who have unusual abilities or difficulties. Two examples of the core studies that are case studies are:

- Thigpen and Cleckley (1954) — individual differences approach; the three faces of Eve.
- Freud (1909)— developmental approach; analysis of Little Hans' phobia.

Advantages

- Gives a rich and detailed picture of an individual and helps to discover how a person's past may be related to their present behaviour.
- Can form a basis for future research.
- By studying the unusual we can learn more about the usual.

Disadvantages

- May rely on memory, which may be inaccurate or distorted.
- Can only inform about one person, so findings can never be generalised.
- The interviewer may be biased and/or the interviewee may not tell the truth.
- Retrospective studies may rely on memory, which may be biased or faulty or incomplete, and past records may be incomplete.

Case studies and ethics

Although consent is gained at the start of a study, ethical issues may arise because the confidentiality and privacy of the participant(s) may be breached if the identity of the person (people) who is being studied is disclosed, or is later 'uncovered'.

Glossary of terms

correlation A statistical technique used to calculate the correlation coefficient in order to quantify the strength of relationship between two variables.

counterbalancing A way of controlling for order effects by having half the participants complete condition A followed by condition B; the other participants complete condition B followed by condition A.

demand characteristics Aspects of the experiment may act as cues to behaviour that cause the participants (and the experimenter) to change the way they behave.

dependent variable (DV) The effect of the IV, or what is measured, in an experiment.

ethical guidelines A set of ethical guidelines for research involving human participants, issued by The British Psychological Society (BPS). These ethical guidelines are designed to protect the wellbeing and dignity of research participants.

external validity The validity of a study outside the research situation and the extent to which the findings can be generalised (ecological validity).

field experiment A way of conducting research in an everyday environment, for example in a school or hospital, where one or more IVs are manipulated by the experimenter and the effect it may have (the DV) is measured.

Hawthorne effect When people are aware that they are being studied, they are likely to try harder on tasks and pay more attention.

hypothesis A hypothesis states precisely what the researcher believes to be true about the target population and is a testable statement.

independent measures design Different participants are used in each of the conditions.

independent variable (IV) The variable that is manipulated (changed) between experimental conditions.

internal validity Whether the IV caused the effect on the DV, or whether some other factor was responsible.

inter-observer reliability If several observers are coding behaviour in an observational study, their codings or ratings should agree with each other.

laboratory experiment A method of conducting research in which researchers try to control all the variables except the one that is changed between the experimental conditions.

matched participants (subjects) design Separate groups of participants are used, matched on a one-to-one basis on characteristics such as age or sex, to control for the possible effect of individual differences.

natural experiment An experimental method, in which, rather than being manipulated by the researcher, the IV to be studied occurs naturally. Some examples of naturally occurring variables are gender and age.

naturalistic observations A research method in which psychologists watch people's behaviour but remain inconspicuous and do nothing to change or interfere with it.

null hypothesis A statement of no difference or of no correlation — the IV does not affect the DV. Tested by the inferential statistical test.

operationalisation of variables Being able to define variables in order to manipulate the IV and measure the DV. For example, performance on a memory test might be operationalised as 'the number of words remembered from a list of words'.

opportunity sampling Asking whoever is available and willing to participate. An opportunity sample is not likely to be representative of any target population because it will probably comprise friends of the researcher, or students, or people in a specific workplace.

order effects When a repeated measures design is used, problems may arise from participants doing the same task twice because the second time they carry out the task, they may be better than the first time because they have had practice, or worse than the first time because they have lost interest or are tired.

qualitative data Rich and detailed data collected in real-life settings, for example people's subjective opinions.

quantitative data Objective, precise, usually numerical data that can be analysed statistically.

random sampling Having the names of the target population and giving everyone an equal chance of being selected.

reliability Consistency of results, that is, if something is measured more than once, the same effect should result.

repeated measures design The same group of participants is used in each of the conditions.

research aim A general statement of the purpose of the study. It should make clear what the study intends to investigate.

self-report method A way of finding out about people's behaviour by interviewing them or by asking them to fill out questionnaires.

social desirability bias When people try to show themselves in the best possible way, so that when answering questions in interviews or questionnaires they give answers that are socially acceptable but are not truthful.

structured interview Participants are asked the same questions in the same order.

validity The extent to which we can be sure that the research measured the effect of what it 'set out to measure' (see also internal validity).

Philip Allan, an imprint of Hodder Education, an Hachette UK company, Market Place, Deddington, Oxfordshire, OX15 0SE

Orders
Bookpoint Ltd, 130 Milton Park, Abingdon, Oxfordshire OX14 4SB
tel: 01235 827827
fax: 01235 400401
e-mail: education@bookpoint.co.uk
Lines are open 9.00 a.m.–5.00 p.m., Monday to Saturday, with a 24-hour message answering service. You can also order through the Philip Allan website: www.philipallan.co.uk

© Molly Marshall 2012
ISBN 978-1-4441-6463-3

First printed 2012

Impression number   5   4   3   2   1
Year   2017   2016   2015   2014   2013   2012

Cover photo reproduced by permission of Sergej Khackimullin/fotolia
Printed in Spain

Hachette UK's policy is to use papers that are natural, renewable and recyclable products and made from wood grown in sustainable forests. The logging and manufacturing processes are expected to conform to the environmental regulations of the country of origin.

P02055

ISBN 978-1-4441-6463-3